SPILLING THE BEANS

A BOOK FOR THE WORLD

by

Rodger Collins

Published in the United States of America by Garden Tree Publishing
4900 Shattuck Avenue #3612, Oakland, CA 94609, United States of America

Edited by Najwa Sabrie, Esq.
Cover Graphics by Michael Angelo Chester and Paul Jones
Concept by Hajji Sabrie

Library of Congress Cataloging-in-Publication Data is available.

ISBN 978-1-957641-04-1 (paperback)
ISBN 978-1-957641-07-2 (hard back)
ISBN 978-1-957641-00-3 (epub-KINDLE)

With the Name of the Most High
The One who creates, but is not created,
I thank The One who loaned me life and then gave me
permission to be aware that I even exist.
I pray for world peace, to be kept in the company of right-
minded people everywhere, and that my mind and my pen
are guided to say what is appropriate in this book.

This book is dedicated to the world.

DISCLAIMER

This book is not intended to be an "I know it and you don't" book. It is simply information. Out of respect for the privacy of individuals, some names may have been omitted or changed.

ABOUT THE BOOK

This book is loaded and a *must-read* filled with gems we overlook. The best description for *Spilling the Beans* is "A Book For
The World." *Spilling the Beans,* relates to good people everywhere. No matter their ethnicity or religion, nor whether they
are female, male, young, old, rich or poor Rodger Collins has
written A Book For The World. In it are gems we casually overlook or take for granted. Many foggy, opaque concepts are
clarified in a style which is easy reading, heartfelt, funny, sad,
educational, refreshing, inspirational, extremely informative,
and motivational.

Spilling the Beans can bring you to tears as it illustrates fairly
and proves *the value of women and girls* is equal to the value of
men and boys. Collins does an excellent job comparing the difference between the bully and the "ain't taking no mess real
man." This book shows how the real man is more than just
some muscles. One short essay, *Young People Go For It,* takes a
sharp look into the huge value, potential and courage of young
people. Long overdue, on its pages are many, many, many more
gems.

In this refreshing work he provides a laser focused search-
light that allows people to see themselves and come to their own
conclusions. When asked, "Why this book?" Collins responded,
"The reason why I wrote this book is because it is needed."

–Alford Nero, retired Fire Chief

ACKNOWLEDGEMENT

A big thank you to everyone who contributed to the success of
Spilling The Beans - A Book For The World
Rodger Collins.

ABOUT THE AUTHOR

Rodger Collins, born in Santa Anna, Texas, has always been very inquisitive about how and why things work. Coupled with his fascination with anthropology and natural sciences, his early rural environment inspired him to observe people and the living things around him. This habit remained with him when his family resettled to the San Francisco Bay Area.

Rodger Collins, author, singer, songwriter, producer, film-maker, and extraordinary entertainer, enjoyed success with the blockbuster recording hit, "She's Looking Good," which went straight to number one on the charts. This was followed by several more hits popular in the United States and internationally. Collins is honored that his works currently continue to sell, are covered by multiple artists on media platforms, and are in commercials.

Collins never stops writing about his vast experiences and rational observations. He has created a masterpiece in this book, *Spilling the Beans*. He has unique insights and a diverse way of expressing them. This author has a lot to share, and this one-of-a-kind powerful book is proof.

He is an honoree with a plaque bearing his name and celebrating his career and music contributions on Oakland's Music Walk of Fame in Oakland, California.

TABLE OF CONTENTS

INTRODUCTION

SERVING UP THE BEANS

This book represents a journey ignited by my life experiences and observations which taught me the importance of curiosity and rational thinking. For example, things taken for granted that are right in front of us that we may overlook, the importance of words and also calling things by their right name. Sometime we can laugh at ourselves when we reflect on our actions and interactions with our fellow human beings.

This collection of beans shares some of the ideas I encountered during my journey and the mingling of our human hearts. It is meant to be thought provoking. It is meant to keep our curiosity excited as we discover our inner self which is one with humanity. Everyone who has lived has something to say about their journey.

In high school I received a four-year acting scholarship, paid for by an alumni Marjorie Steele, after she was impressed by my performance in a school play that she attended. Steele was the famed actress of the hit play, "Cat on a Hot Tin Roof." This scholarship was to the Actor's Lab in San Francisco under the skilled direction of Mara Alexander Gilbert. The acting skills I acquired were fundamental in shaping my ability to get into characters when I write and perform on stage. This training enhanced all of my creative ability and skill to use improvisations to bring characters to life. My appreciation for this experience is unmeasurable.

I observed how some of the world's greatest entertainers have the ability to take the audience on a journey of emotions, the highs and the lows, and through it all tap into the humanity they share with their audience. You may have a similar journey as you travel through this serving of *Spilling the Beans*. Buckle up, we're about to take off!

–Rodger Collins

THE OPENING

BUCKLE UP, WE'RE ABOUT TO TAKE OFF!

WAKING UP

Waking up is not an absolutely quick process. Always remember, a person doesn't wake up all of a sudden. No matter how fast we wake up, we must do it in stages.

Everyone in the room knows that the sleeping one is waking up before the sleeping one does. No matter who we are, we have to walk one step at a time. We see the dawn before we see the bright sun.

I see all of these wonderful people waking up. At last, at last, at last, it appears that the beginning of the new world is here. The chance of a lifetime is here. Never allow your enemy to train you. And be careful so that you don't become a watchman for the boss. Education indeed costs a lot. But being uninformed and/or being misinformed costs much, much more.

DIS-COVER (remove the cover).

Yea-a-a-a, waking up is fun!

Beans Spilled.

KEYS TO FREEDOM

The keys to real freedom, for all people, lie inside language(s). Unlocking languages and calling things by their correct name is a joy and a must.

Example:

Dome: The top of the anatomy; the head, the mind, and/ or the brain. A silent "e" on "dome" gives us "dom." Free the dome, *free-dome*. So, "freedom" means . . . free *the mind*.

SCHOLASTIC AND PRACTICAL

B oth are very important but neither is the best. The combination, both thoroughly mixed together, is the very best and that'll get you to the top of the logical pyramid.

⊷⟾◠⟽⊶

EYE-OPENER

W hen I went to get my COVID-19 shot, a woman helping with filling out the short intake forms politely asked me, "What's your race?" Without hesitation, I said, "Human. What other race can I be? I can't be a giraffe."

We'll talk more about this subject later in the book.

IT TAKES ONE TO KNOW ONE

C an a person with a good heart recognize the good heart in someone else? There's a simple method to identify a person with a good heart. The person with a good heart has a special glow and sparkles in their eyes. If we're also good—it can stir our hearts and souls as no others can when good people speak. Imitators may come close, but this pure, good-hearted person, with their original human nature, has an edge.

All babies are born with that same goodness. Some abandon it, whereas others keep it for life. People who abandon their original, sweet, precious human nature may never be able to identify the ones who kept it. The ones who kept it may feel a sense of loneliness and can recognize other good-hearted people right away. They might say, "Oh my goodness! There's another one like me." *It takes one to know one.*

WE'RE ALL WE GOT

Not long ago, a complete stranger helped me load a large item into my car. When I thanked him, his reply was heart-felt. He said, "I had to help you, man. We're all we got." I never forgot that.

I've heard people say that we don't have everything the way that we want it here. Well, what do you say about us getting together and fixing it if we're supposed to be as smart as we think we are? What if we all do our part? If we can all appreciate love, why not love each other?

What do you say about us applying the same mindset of that stranger toward one big global family? I often think of that man who gave me that hand because, when it comes to our human family interactions toward each other, he was right, *we're all we got.*

I just spilled some beans.

QUESTION: THE MEANING OF "OPINION"?

What's the difference between personal opinion and reason?

Here we go: "Personal opinion" simply means something that a person seriously believes with absolutely no proof (**weak**.)

"Reason" is all of the scientific evidence—proven evidence— gathered. When this evidence is put together (without anyone's "personal opinion" included), this evidence can give or lead to the correct conclusion (**strong**.)

Personal opinion is merely a guess. It's a bluff (**very weak**.)

Reason is what proof is (**super strong**.)

Beans Spilled.

BRAINWASHED

A brainwashed person will never go near the question of, "How do I know if I'm brainwashed?" I did an investigation on this matter.

I went to a professor, and I asked, "How does a person know for sure if they're brainwashed?" The professor said, "Well, the person might be suffering from anxiety, or it could be the buoyancy of the diversity of the matriculation of the antidisestablishmentarianism, or something of that nature."

I thanked the professor, then I went to a wino.

I asked the wino the same question: "How can a person tell for sure if they're brainwashed?"

The wino said, "That's easy! It's easy to know if you're brainwashed."

I asked, "How's that?"

He said, "YOU'RE STUPID." **Bingo! I mean B-I-N-G got dern GO.**

I thanked him and thought to myself, "Hmmm, things that make you think."

DETERMINATION

I s it true that every baby naturally knows how to apply effort? Should we all observe what a baby does naturally? We don't have to teach a baby to *try*.

We're all human. We all make serious mistakes, but it's natural to try again. We each get a chance to try and make the best of life.

It's common knowledge that every baby can't even turn over without, applied effort. However, after a baby turns over *just once*, it can turn over again and again anytime it wants to do so.

After learning how to roll over, a baby must then learn how to sit up. To accomplish this, babies must try. *Here comes that effort again!* The baby tries and tries and tries until it can finally sit up. After one time of sitting up, the baby knows how to do it and immediately sets another goal . . . standing.

Do you think a baby quits when it's struggling to learn how to stand up? *No way!* Effort again kicks into gear until it can stand up.

Now the baby can easily roll over, sit up, and stand up. Hey, wait a minute! There's trouble . . . the baby can't walk. It quickly goes back into its reserve of determination. The baby tries and tries, it fails sometimes, and it tries some more. Then *bingo!* Wow, the first step. Soon the baby is walking, jumping, and running.

We were all babies once before and had to experience that determination, remember? This principle continues throughout our lives. We should never forget that. When the trials of life occur, that's when we should stop, study our directions, reflect, and try again. Then once again we'll be on our way! The baby shows each and every one of us that we can do it if we try.

THE LIAR

Many wonderful people with good intentions sometimes spread incorrect information. These people are **definitely not liars.** *They believe what they're spreading or saying is correct.* **But the liar is different.** *He or she is lying to deceive or to mislead.*

Here is an example of confronting a liar:

"Hey sneak! First, you said your daddy was a rock star, then you said he was a surgeon, now you want folks to believe your mama is a virgin.

Liar, that's just unacceptable! Liar, this might strike you as a terrible blow, you have a whole lot of class, "charmer", BUT IT'S ALL LOW.

You will lie about anything. I'm told that we have to earn trust because trust don't come free. Your reputation is horrendous. You are such a crook. Before trusting you again, we have to think about dropping our guards. Trusting you again may be a bad decision, liar. We have to really, really think. Believing anything you have to say would be like placing a vampire in charge of inventory at the blood bank. You are a deceiver. You lie with a straight face. But that's not all you do, you'll lie when you are crying. You are just not to be trusted, because you lie all the time. That's your profile.

NOW, THAT DESCRIBES A LIAR.

LIAR! YOU'LL LIE ABOUT ANYTHING

(SONG LYRICS WRITTEN AND RECORDED BY RODGER COLLINS)

L iar! you'll lie about anything. First, you said your daddy was a rockstar, and then you said he was a surgeon, *now you're trying to make folks believe, that your mama is a virgin.* Your words are sweet like sugar but they're just not ringing true. We can't believe a word you say because we see what you do. The cat's out the bag. The cat's out the bag on you. Since the sun got to showing, your coattail sure is blowing. Liar! You'll lie about anything. Cat's out the bag on you.

Gave you all the trust we could but, you returned our trust with pain, pouring water down our back trying to tell us that it's rain. Every ear is buzzing so don't even ask for pity. We're too hip to the kat to get tricked by the kitty. The cat's out the bag. Ahhh you rascal, you! The cat's out the bag on you. Meow! Everyone knows that you're not right. How does it feel sleeping in the spotlight? Liar! You'll lie about anything. Cat's out the bag on you.

Wrong with your guilty look written all over your face. You're caught with your hand in the cookie jar, so now I rest my case. Goodbye, you know you're wrong and now the panic is on. Reaching in your big black bag but, your magic is gone. The cat's out the bag. Meow! Ahhh you rascal, you! The cat's out the bag on you. No matter what you do, your little game is through. Liar! You'll lie about anything. Cat's out the bag on you.

Running like an Olympic star trying to cover up the truth. You lying son of a gun, everyone knows that you're trying to hide on the roof. Liar! You'll lie about anything.

MISS RATTLER

O ne day in San Francisco, I saw a boy disrespecting his mother, hurting her so badly, and he said to her, "I didn't ask to come here."

I asked her, "Miss Rattler, may I say something to that boy?" She said, "Yes."

I said, "Boy, you not only asked to come here, but you also fought to come here. When your mother and father had sexual intercourse, from 15 to 200 million sperm were released. Guess who elbowed his way past all of his brothers and sisters, and made it to that egg so that he could fertilize it? YOU! And now that she suffered and got you here, you got what you wanted. Now you don't want what you got. You'd better think about that. Yes, you better check yourself before you be by yourself."

Just spilling a few beans with you.

NAKED SPORTS

Running down the track, wind blowing, butt showing—do I have to show my crack to run track?

It's just too immoral.

Do I have to be naked to play volleyball?

Who makes these rules? These are the rules, of course, but I don't want to get naked just to play sports.

Looks like, to me, somebody's faking.

What do you think?
Beans . . .

⊷⟞⟝⊶

I HAVE A FRIEND

I have a friend, and I know they're a friend. My heart asked, "If you're right, produce your proof." I'm happy to; their track record speaks for itself.

ALONZO'S ADVICE

M y cousin, Alonzo, told me, "Try to never cause a person to lose their job because you never know who's waiting and/or depending on that check at the other end. Always remain considerate. With an unmistakable appreciative expression on his face Alonzo continued to say, "I'm so grateful that my father, Willie Brown, instilled that in me."

⋅⊱══⊙ ⊙══⊰⋅

BLACK CAT

D id you ever look for something and couldn't find it because you already had it?

Remember, whenever we find something that we're looking for, it's always in the last place we look. That's why we found it. It was the last place we looked. It can be like a blind man in a dark room, looking for a black cat that's not even in there.

PEDAL TONES

When I was a boy in the little country town of Santa Anna, Texas I observed how we relied on each other for help. I took my younger daughter to visit so one of her dreams would be fulfilled. She wanted to see where I was born and raised. We visited the house where I lived and went up the stairs and took pictures in the room where I was born. We went outside where I played as a child, and visited the little church of which I often spoke. After visiting these sites, she and I could see and feel more of what I experienced as a boy.

Each hug and handshake, some I knew from when I was growing up and some were from new people we were meeting, was heartfelt. These were the kinds of hugs and handshakes you can't buy. I said to my daughter, "Wow baby, just look at this. They're still doing it, never forget this. They all treat each other just like family."

My inner self inspired me to compose this, "Human beings are *pedal tones* in the universal harmony of chords *played in the most magnificent symphony* called GOD'S Mighty Creation."

Can we all agree on this and say... "Now, that's human family!"

READ THE LABELS

UNSALTED TOP CRACKERS

When people read the label of unsalted top crackers, they sometimes misunderstand it to mean there's no salt in the cracker's ingredients. This is not the correct interpretation of the unsalted top cracker label.

Unsalted top crackers *do* have salt in them; however, they *do not* have salt sprinkled on top. That's why they're called unsalted *top* crackers.

Read the ingredients carefully and, *bingo!* The ingredients do say there *is* salt! Unsalted **top** crackers mean just what it says . . .

UNSALTED TOP!

FROM CONCENTRATE

D o we ever notice the words, "pure unsweetened **from** concentrate" on the juice labels we buy? First, let's be absolutely clear on what concentrate is. Concentrate is a thick syrup that is usually loaded with sugar and other sweeteners. Are we sure that we're getting unsweetened juice when it says unsweetened *from* concentrate on the label? The key word here is "from". If it said unsweetened, and nothing else, great. But *"from concentrate"* could mean that it was *sweetened before it became concentrated* or during the process of being concentrated. Unsweetened **from** concentrate doesn't mean that it was never sweetened; it only means that after being concentrated it has not been sweetened further.

Whoops! 100-percent pure unsweetened *from* concentrate can be misleading. How was it before it became *concentrated?*

LAUNDRY DETERGENTS

L aundry detergent is a combination of mixing cleaner and suds. Many people believe that suds do the cleaning but the cleaner can clean very well without making suds. Suds do not clean; instead, they exist to make the customers happy just through their appearance.

I was informed by a national appliance instructor that, a month after powder laundry detergent is opened, it loses its potency. It can still make suds, *but it can't clean as well.*

Beans Spilled.

MYSTERIOUS CHAMPIONS

Person 1: *The "Breakfast of Champions"*
Person 2: *Champions of who, or what?*
Person 1: *I don't know, do you?*

LIFETIME GUARANTEE

Often a lifetime guarantee is offered when we make a purchase. The lifetime guarantee of what? Oh, I see, not *the buyer's* lifetime, the lifetime of the *product* is guaranteed.

Hmm, what if something is wrong with the product in a week? Is the "lifetime" guarantee finished? We must read the fine print very carefully to know what is actually guaranteed.

It's good to call things by their right names, and, by all means, read the fine print!

COULD IT BE THE SUGAR?

I said, *oooow*! This food is just fantastic, the taste is just fantastic. I've never tasted food this delicious. What did you put in this food to make it taste so good?

All of the cooks and chefs (family included), person-to-person, basically told me the same thing. "I don't tell what I put in my food." They said, "I don't share my recipes, nor how I prepare my food, with *anyone*. That's a trade secret." They were all zipped lipped.

So, I became convinced that this trade secret must be really special. I started pondering, really wondering. *What can it be?*

Lips are smacking, taste buds kicking, can't hardly wait for some more fried chicken. Aunt Minnie's soul food, Little Sister's cornbread, Mr. Jake, just put a hurting on these bar-b-que ribs. I'm cleaning these ribs, down to the bone, can't leave 'em alone.

I said *ooooh*, this food tastes so good, I wonder why? A little voice inside of me whispered and said, *"They put sugar in almost everything, I'm told."*

"Not the 'que," I said.

"Yes, the que," the little voice said, *"and the gumbo too!"*

I asked, *"Is that right?"*

The little voice came back again and whispered, *"Could it be the sugar, sugar, sugar, sugar? Could it be the sugar? It just might be the sugar."*

My burrito, my taco, and my enchiladas? Mmmm, deliciosa!

My chop suey, my Szechuan beef, my shrimp-fried-rice, Ni Hao Ma (*thank you!*), Bu Ke Qi (*you're welcome!*). I got to have my meatballs, my spaghetti, and my lasagna (*Arrivederci!*)

I must have a jones. I can't stop. I'm hooked, I might drop. Taste so good, it's a fact. If I stop eating, my stomach might think I'm cheating. This tasty food has me going, "*I wonder why?*"

The little voice inside my head whispered again. It said, "*They put sugar in almost everything, I'm told.*"

I replied again, "*Is that right?*"

The little voice repeated, "*It might be the sugar, sugar, sugar, sugar. Could it be the sugar? It just might be the sugar.*"

It's sugar all over the place. Cakes, pies, cookies, chips, donuts, candy, collard greens, hamburgers, french fries, sodas, hotdogs, ice cream, popsicles, seafood, jelly, coffee, jam, cereal, soup, milk, hot chocolate, sweet tea.

Oooh, my toothache, these cavities are killing me, and my diabetes, my sugar diabetes.

OUCH!

Did I overdo it?

Hmmm, interesting . . .

THE MIGHTY COLOR RED

The color red is the strongest and most unique of all colors. The slightest dot of the color red is strong enough to raise the heartbeat and excite emotions. The color red is like no other color.

A little red dot is so powerful it can make us pay attention unconsciously and often leads us to make purchases. Maybe that's why it's so successfully used in marketing. The color red is used as an extremely effective tool in TV and internet marketing because it can get attention like no other color.

When we go into the supermarket, we notice that almost everything has that red on it. When we look in the kitchen, almost everything in the kitchen cabinets has some red on it. Letters, numbers, and/or designs. On spice cans, bottles, and boxes, there is going to be some red—it may be the *tiniest* little dot. The same thing may appear on a loaf of bread or bag of cookies.

The color red is also used in tail lights, signal lights, stop signs, flashing police lights, and on fire engines and their flashing lights. Bullfighters always use a red cape to confuse the bull's decisions with high emotions. The slightest sight of blood can sometimes make people faint because it excites their emotions.

Many times, when we read something and it's talking about red, it is referring to allegorical language used to create red hot emotions. The saying often goes, "I was so upset, I was *seeing red*" because the color red is very, very powerful.

So, there we have it—an explosive look at the tremendous influence of the mighty color red.

Beans Spilled.

YOUNG PEOPLE, GO FOR IT

YOUNG PEOPLE, GO FOR IT

F irst, I give thanks to the Most High for allowing me to see the good in young people that I see. This essay is dedicated to young people everywhere I am very inspired by young people. I love and respect young people. They teach me lots of new things. They're great, I talk to them at length nearly every day. I hear them out and sincerely listen to what they have to say. Wow, they really have some valuable things to say. *However, one thing I've noticed is that they all say that no one listens to them.* **Well, I do!**

I generally start out by asking them, *"If there was something that you wanted to say to an older person what would it be besides, 'leave me alone'"?* They immediately recognize me as a friend and welcome me into their heads. I'm rolling with them because I feel young people's pain and loneliness.

I must share this universal information that is right under our noses to my young friends *around the world.* No matter if it's young teenagers or young adults. Please take your time and read it. It may be a big help and encourage all to do in depth research.

Some young people in this world don't have it as rough as others. Some people are pampered. Too much pampering is not good. Some people get everything done for them. No, no, no a baby trying to learn how to walk will push your hand away and try to learn without any help. The baby's actions and great determination are saying, "Let me do it myself".

Sometimes a young person is hurt so badly that they can barely have a full recovery. They are so depressed but they have determination and can fight their way to recovery. Don't ever feel like you are at the very bottom with no way out. **That's an illusion.** *Our built-in determination tells us better than that.*

I've heard some parents talk to their children like this, "I hate your little behind", "I wish I would have never had you", "I wish you'd never been born." And that child is crying pitifully.

Parents, do you know what you just did? Do you *really* know what you just did?

Parents, I'm speaking to you: Do those parents know how they just hurt this helpless child by saying that? Not to mention the filthy swear words these parents might be using.

Now this might surprise you but some parents might not even know the damage they just caused because they might still be suffering from a traumatic hangover where somebody did that exact same thing to them and they innocently passed it on to an innocent child, scarring them for life. This child is hurt beyond description. They are sometimes surprised and can't understand why someone they love and trust would talk to them like that. Often, they are punished just because they tried something and made a mistake. Well they are totally new to this world and they are going to make many mistakes. So, let's be kind and gentle with young people. Let's respect them and give them more chances.

Let's give that child that feels down at the bottom some encouragement. We must realize that they have never been in this world before. Young people are new to this world. They are here for the first time and they are trying to find their way. They don't need people pushing them around.

To all adults let's not forget that once we too were young and all young folks are trying to figure out this thing called life.

I'm attempting to show how one can possibly make it all the way to the top with one's own efforts. When determination appears to be gone it isn't. It is still there. Natural determination is still inside of us just waiting for us to use it. We just have to find it and apply it.

I repeat this to all youngsters, we came in this world with some determination that's hard to see sometimes but we have it. We came all the way from a sperm and beyond to the point of conception where from 15 to 200 million sperm were released. Only one sperm out of those millions made it to the egg in the mother's body, fertilized that egg and formed a fetus. That fetus grows into the physical baby we see. And it can come all the way up to become a successful adult. But we have to start by learning the importance of what's inside of us.

Shouldn't our heart be with the youth and I say to them, "You're our future. Go for all that's good. Never, ever think you can't do it. You have too much courage for that. If you have a bright idea, go for it. Shoot for the top. *Don't go for baloney.* Reach for the top. Never let your opponent mess with your brain, peeing down your back, trying to tell you it's rain. Always, always, always call things by their right names, then you can see better where you're going. You don't need a weather-forecaster to tell you which way the wind's blowing. You already have it in you, everything you need to make you superior to whoever you're looking up to. We just have to be aware that it's there. So young people go for it. If you're going to do it, get to it. Do it!

Time waits for no one. Don't wait too long because time will pass you by, and then it will be gone. Go for it now. Get to it. Young people, you can bring your vision of a better world into reality. **Just don't make the mistake and let your enemy train you.**"

YOUR TIME IS NOW!

Who knows, you youngsters may make it all the way to the top, come up with a new concept and re-orchestrate society. I believe in you because you have a lot of what you need already in you. You have a lot in you that some old folks may not have. You have energy, you have courage, **you are not afraid**. With a keen universal focus one can make better decisions with stronger plans and higher commitments. Once we learn the right patterns, who knows, it could be you that change the world. It just might be you that establishes real fairness and makes it popular around the world. **The original world is designed to welcome you.**

YOUNG PEOPLE GO FOR IT!

We were sent here to learn. After arriving helpless in this life, we must accept some help and guidance from others. However, **never forget** what each baby did on its own. The baby learned to turn over for the first time from its own efforts. **Wow**, that is some *striving!* There is also something else that's fantastic about you, and that's action. Young people you have action. You create action. You're busy. You're a diamond in the rough. To all youngsters, female and male, go for it worldwide. Go for it. Think first then act. **Don't over-rush but don't drag. Go for all that's good, and with all you've got.**

I was shown that everybody can excel at something. Never think that you're on the bottom. No mater what one's personality is, watch what they do; that expresses the real person. Do you agree that it's best to be good and that includes never accepting BS?

The sky is the limit; it's a must, not a steal. But if you don't grab opportunities and orchestrate society, somebody else will. **You're in position for the mission.**

*This song is included with the intentions of describing the deep sentiments of some parents who have tried everything they know about raising children and still missed the mark. Let's remember most parents were young also and trying to find their way when the children were born.

Before reviewing the lyrics to Just One More Time what do you say about this consideration? Let's not put the cause on the child, children, or parents. **The cause may just be a misunderstanding.**

JUST ONE MORE TIME

(SONG LYRICS WRITTEN AND RECORDED BY RODGER COLLINS)
Go to www.spillingthebeans.com to listen to the audio

I t's so heavy on me, it's on me so heavy, you see
Our son was led astray by his friends and their foolish charms
Oh, I wished, I wished I could have found you and
Rescued you from troubles' arms
It was a pain the way you, the way you lost your life
You were just living in a fool's paradise
(But I love you anyway)
And I'd love to see you one more time
(And its heavy on me)
If I could hold you in my arms like I hold you in my mind
(It's heavy)
Then baby, son, daddy would be happy one more time
(It's heavy)
Oh, I know you're gone to never return
(vocalization)
And maybe someday in the future I'll stop crying
(vocalization)
And I'll be happy one more time

(vocalization)
I'm still working hard, your mom's a busy bee
(vocalization)
It's a family situation
You're heavy on our hearts, the pain is striking deep
(vocalization)
It's a family situation
(vocalization)
Our daughter ran away with a boy
Who plays with her life like a toy
In a dream a few nights ago
I saw her standing somewhere wondering which way to go
Well now if ESP can work for me
I hope it will find her and bring her back home to the family
Cause I'd love to see you one more time
(And it's heavy on me)
If I could hold you in my arms like I hold you in my mind
(Heavy)
Then baby, daddy would be happy one more time
(And it's heavy on me)
I'd like to see you one more time
(And it's heavy on me)
Just one more time
(vocalization)

ROAD RAGE YOU GONNA DO **WHAT**?

O ne peaceful day I waited at a signal light. Out of nowhere, this wild, crazy guy skidded around me while he cursed me out and called me a motherf—ker. I quickly pulled up beside him in the next block. I let my window down and apologized to him. He was still arrogant and thought he had me. I said, "Man, I'm so sorry." He shouted back and asked disrespectfully and arrogantly, "Sorry about what, motherf--ker?" I said, "You called me a motherf--ker, and I owe you an apology. I'm so sorry. I had no idea that that was your mama." He became extremely upset and started shouting even more. I calmly responded by saying, "No need to be so upset. I'm glad to finally meet you, son." He burned rubber as he drove off. So, I guessed by then he's probably saying to himself, "Oh well, I guess I can't win them all."

So, I went on about my peaceful day.

BE CAREFUL

A friend of mine told me, "You'd better be careful out here." I asked, "Why, what's wrong?"

My friend said, "A guy who I always thought was a friend of mine came to me and said, 'Let me hold $20.'"

My friend replied, "Sure."

His buddy said, "Hold up, don't give me that $20, man. Just give me $10 now, and now you owe me $10."

When his buddy left, my friend said to himself, "Wait a minute! I loaned him $10, but I owe him $10? That sneak! We're even. *He just got me!*"

My friend told me that he's more awake now, more on guard. He said, "I was in a service station and a panhandler came up to me and asked, 'Would you let me have $15 for a cup of coffee.'" My friend snapped at him and said, "I'm not giving you anything. You know that a cup of coffee doesn't cost $15." The panhandler said, "Oh, I know that, but I'm a heavy tipper." My friend said, "Well I'm not giving you anything; how about that?"

My friend proceeded to tell me that he went to a coffee shop to collect his thoughts. The coffee was terrible, so he complained to the waitress. The waitress returned with the owner. The owner said, "I don't appreciate you talking bad about our coffee. My friend replied, "Well I don't like your terrible coffee." With a relaxed demeanor, the owner said, "Let me put it this way: stop complaining about our coffee because you may be old and weak your own self one day."

My friend told me, "So you see, Rodger, it's all over the place! *Be careful, man,* because it's not easy out here, life is filled with next."

SEARCHING FOR ME
(WITH A FLASHLIGHT IN THE DAY TIME)

I love the best of humanity but I didn't know that I could know me. I could tell that I was somewhere, but I didn't quite know where. I would look into the mirror and say, "Are you in there?"

I would lie in the bed at night and ask, "Where are you?" Seems like a little voice inside would say, "You'll know, you'll remember "me" when the time is right (just keep trying.)" Then when I least expected it, here I am. Here I am meeting me again.

Should I tell everybody and be bold or should I just be grateful and say, "Me is the soul." At last, now I remember. Howdy soul! Good to see you again.

A CLOSER LOOK

I t's rewarding to get to know the complexities of our makeup. Sometimes, we get distracted and forget about our real core. During some investigations, I discovered that a huge number of us only like or love a few things: entertainment; getting high (it's *really* low); good feelings (stimulated by sex, bright colors, bright lights, sounds); fun; TV (*Tell-A-Vision*); eating too much unhealthy, good-tasting food; and a handful of other things.

All of us know we must use the bathroom, but do we care to know what takes place inside our bodies for us to do it? Just drinking a glass of water or digesting some food through our body is a major process.

We all love the good feelings of sex, but do we ever think about, or even care what takes place inside our bodies to bring about those wonderful feelings? When a man has an erection, does he even care to know what takes place inside of his body for that to happen?

It is a thrilling experience to learn more about our human make up. In the next few sections of this book, we're going to have a look at a few more important things often overlooked about the way humans work. Hope you like it.

What is "self"?

It's not me. *Self is different than me.* "Self" is the character. Self is one's independent identity. It refers to one's personality, and expressions. These are all dimensions of the mind that are made up of life experiences, strengths, and preferences to form one's independent identity.

Wouldn't you say that it's exciting to meet ourselves?

So now we have it, we know what self is.

Beans Spilled.

WHAT IS NATIONALITY?

A Common Mistake Corrected

Nationality **is not** race (human), a person (the mind), or an ethnicity (culture). Nationality **is the origin** of one's birth, and/or the country in which one is a registered member.

Example: If one is born in *America,* their nationality is *American.* If one is born in *Mexico,* their nationality is *Mexican.* If one is born in Canada, their nationality is *Canadian.*

However, if one is born in a country and then later becomes a registered citizen of another country, that person's nationality is of *both* countries.

Mexican-American,
Pakistani-American,
Nigerian-American,
Irish-American,
Chinese-American,
French-Canadian,
and more

For example, if the registered citizen has a baby born in their new country the **baby's nationality is the name of the new country.**

So, what is nationality? The origin of one's birth and or where they are a registered citizen.

WE ALL HAVE A ME

E arlier in *Spilling the Beans* we discovered the meaning of *self* and also the meaning of *me*. Would you say this is just plain, good stuff? How do we get to know that *me* discovered is really *me*? What is some proof?

The voice inside of us that is constantly whispering, "Do this, or don't do that." It doesn't force, it just suggests. When we don't accept the suggestion and get into trouble, each time we say, "Something told me not to do that". It's the main part of us that we ignore sometime. Everyone knows about the whispering voice inside and somehow everyone at times forgets or ignores it. But when the time was right like a bolt of thunder and a streak of heat, pow! There it is, *ME*.

Me is purpose, *me* is also described as original human nature and as stated earlier it can also be called the soul.

The beans have been spilled!

⊷⟾◑ ◒⟽⊶

WHAT IS ETHNICITY?

E thnicity refers to the habits or similarities developed among a group or groups (e.g., food, clothing, entertainment). Ethnicity means *culture*.

WHAT IS A PERSON?

Question: What is a person?
Answer: *The rational mind* (a dimension of the human.)

"P er" means "each," "independent," and/or "individual." "Son" or "sun" here represents the same thing: light, awareness, knowledge—simply, *the mind.*

So here, "per-son" represents "each (rational) mind." Each human has one. Person simply means the individual mind.

The rational mind begins when the umbilical cord is cut. As soon as the fetus (the baby's body) exits the mother's body and the umbilical cord is cut, we say, "the baby is born!" That means that rational thinking has started. The baby begins learning when it reads its surroundings by collecting information—light, pictures, words, sounds, experiences, and much, much more—to be stored for later use. This operation is the mind being formed.

"Person" simply means the rational mind of an individual.

WHAT IS RACE?

Question: What is one's race?
Answer: *Human.*

Human is the highest form of creation that is composed of spiritual, physical and mental dimensions. We humans are only one species. We are all the same underneath the skin.

not White,
not Black,
not African-American,
not Caucasian,
not Asian,
not Hispanic,
not any other ethnic group or nationality.

That's why there is only one race (human). The proper name is *homo sapiens.* A cat has many species — tigers, house cats, lions, cheetahs, and so on. Birds also have several species—eagles, hummingbirds, sparrows, parrots, etc. Lizards have over *six thousand* species. We, humans, have only one species: human. **Why keep fighting over something that doesn't exist (a waste of time)?** Why keep believing that there is more than one race? We're all the same human but not the same person. We discussed "person" in the earlier selection of this book called "What is a person?"

If we take the hearts out of two human beings and lay them side by side, we would see they are two human hearts.

Beans, Beans, Beans Spilled.

TAKING A LIFE

N o matter who, no matter when, can we think again? It's not our life, so why take it? Everyone has a chance, but that chance gets lost if that life is taken. Every day in this life, we're trying to make it. *Going for it, going for it,* life's journey is snatched away, gone forever when it's taken.

Did we think, did one really think, before they took a life?

In the heat of raging emotions, that thought at the moment was small. But it appeared huge; it appeared big. But when one takes a life, look at what was done. Was it worth it? *Was it really worth it?*

Beans Spilled.

NAME-CALLING

P erhaps we've been known to say how much we love our precious little offspring, but let's have a look at how some offspring are talked to sometimes.

"You little snot."

"Hi, dookie."

"Get your hands off that, you little s-h-i-t."

"Get in there and watch TV (Tell-a-vision: shaping one's
perception, telling one what to learn) before I kick your little
behind. And don't get that on my couch, stinky."

(When company comes) It might change, it might be "Do
you love me, boo?"

Or one might say, "Oh, I love you, poop!"

Or, "Come here, dog."

"Shut up, fart face."

Or saying to the child, "You're just like your darn daddy."

Or saying to the child, "You're just like your stupid mother."

Could we be looking at a little bit of two-face here? Hmmm,
just a thought.

Can we live up to the title of parents in charge of shaping
tomorrow's leaders and tomorrow's parents? I must grab my
own self by the collar and say, "Look, self! Check yourself."

"Who, me?"

"Yes, you."

OOPS! MISSED THE POINT

A friend of mine was telling me about a co-worker out on his job whose personality changed drastically in one day. All of a sudden, he strangely started ordering everyone around; "Move this, move that, take this in, take that out." So, my friend approached him and inquired, "Hey man, what's up with you? Why are you acting this way?" He answered in an arrogant voice, "I'm on the Advisors' Committee now! I got promoted up to a high position. I can tell folks what to do now. The Boss respects my opinion. I'm going to get paid for what I know."

"How do you know for sure that you've been promoted?" my friend asked. He answered in his new smart aleck voice, "The boss himself promoted me. It was early this morning. I was talking to him, telling him some things that I think need to be done differently around here, this that and the other. The boss was so impressed until he put his hands up and stopped me in my tracks. 'Wait a minute, hold up,' he said, and **right then** *he put me on the advisors' committee.*"

The boss said, **"Let's get this straight right now; if I need your advice, I'll ask you."**

My friend said that he looked at his co-worker and then said, "Oops!"

EDUCATION

Did you know: Although education is expensive, being *un*informed, and/or *mis*informed costs much, *much* more? Would you agree an education with a universal scope makes it easier to navigate through life successfully?

If someone teaches a person how to drive a car, they don't necessarily have to teach that person where to go in the car. If one is taught **how to learn** it is easier to see **what to learn**.

MISS FRANKLIN

I 'm a "why guy." I like to know why this and why that. I just don't like to stop until I know how it works. But, as a teenager, when I came from Texas to California and went to high school, my "whys" came to an abrupt, temporary pause.

I hated history, and I disliked Miss Franklin, my history teacher, even more. She begged us students to settle down, get history under our belts, and learn it from different angles. It seemed like daily she told us that history is important. She would tell us, "Please don't ignore this. You're going to need to know history later to help you navigate your way through life better." I couldn't stand it. I didn't like it. I was irritated. I hated history, and I was annoyed by Miss Franklin.

As an adult, my "whys" returned, and I became curious again. My variety of life experiences and observations had encouraged me to learn, embrace, and appreciate history more. My awareness of history increased from many angles, and I often thought about our history teacher, who we thought was so crazy, stupid, and mean. Much older and mature now, my "whys" are on fire more than ever.

Now guess what? As I was driving down Polk Street one day in San Francisco, there standing at the bus stop was a little old lady. She appeared to be about 90 to 95 years old. I said to myself, "Hold up, stop! That looks like it could be Miss Franklin."

I pulled into the end of the bus zone. I hopped out and rushed over to the little old lady and gently and respectfully asked her, "Would your name be Miss Franklin?"

She softly replied, "Yes."

I asked, "Were you a history teacher at Poly High?"

She replied, "Yes."

I said, "Miss Franklin, my name is Rodger Collins, and I was one of your students."

She said very heartfelt (like a mother), "I remember you, Rodger."

I said, "Miss Franklin, I hated history, and I didn't like you at the time. But I learned to love studying and examining history, and I learned to double love and appreciate you. Your words and your sincere efforts stayed with me. I stand tall and proud to say today that I love and appreciate you and what you tried so hard to get us students to see. I want you to know that your efforts weren't lost. Now that I know to love and appreciate your wonderful heart and endurance, can I give you a big hug?"

Miss Franklin responded, "I would love a big hug from you, Rodger."

I gave her the biggest hug I could give, a hug like you would give your mother.

As I was standing there, holding back tears, I said, "I didn't know the value of you in high school, but I know now how to properly appreciate and respect you. I thank you for trying so hard to give all us students a treasure from your heart."

She thanked me.

As I left, we waved at each other; it was a seal to another "why." Maybe that's the reason why we're given tear ducts, so that we may have a joyous cry.

Wow, what an experience! Now, for me, it's right off the bat on a brand-new journey to a brand new "why."

RIGHT OFF THE BAT

The expression "right off the bat" means just getting started.
It doesn't say, the ball stayed connected to the bat. In fact,
it means the opposite, that the ball is just leaving the bat. So,
"right off the bat" means . . .

. . . the beginning of a new journey.

HOPSCOTCH

I f you look Scotch up in the dictionary you will find the following meaning:

(n.) Scots[1].

The definitions for Scots:

(adj.) of or relating to Scotland or its people
(n.) the English language of Scotland

Now, let's look at the term "hopscotch." This is literally saying *bypass the Scots*, or *hop over them*. Although that's what it's *saying*; let's hope that's not what it *means*. The term "hopscotch" sounds like it might need to be reexamined and rethought.

We will learn later in the book that words make people. We can't think of anything unless we give it a *name*. Where did "hopscotch" come from? Why teach this term to unsuspecting little ones? Wow, what do you think?

---

[1] Merriam-Webster.com.

THE MIRROR

H ave you ever wondered what makes some people so arrogant and antisocial? It may simply be *the mirror.* Too much time in the mirror can make us unreasonably admire our image. Then we may begin to worship our bodies. When that happens, we lose focus and forget about the real jewels, which are inside of ourselves.

SMART LITTLE BOY

My neighbor, Sherman, asked a little boy, "What's the most important finger on your hand?"

The little boy answered and said, "My thumb."

Sherman asked the little boy, "Why do you say it's your thumb?"

The little boy said, "Because if I didn't have my thumb, I couldn't eat my peanut butter and jelly sandwich!"

Good thinking little fella.

Now that's a smart little boy!

⊷⇒◉ ⟆⊷

SMART TEENAGER

Another young person who knows something too:
I asked a young man, about 17 or 18 years old, if he knew what he was.

He replied, "Yes."

I asked him, "What?"

He replied "BROKE!"

THE REAL MEANING OF UNDERSTANDING

"Understanding" is an important word that perhaps we all use. There are two parts to the word "understanding." The first part "under" indicates underneath, and the second part, "standing," can indicate that something is remaining in force protecting what is precious and valuable underneath.

Example: Envision a bucket turned upside down and placed on top of some precious diamonds. Here, the diamonds represent "under" and the bucket represents "standing" or protection. So, underneath the bucket is where the valuable diamonds are.

Can we now see how important it is to look underneath something covered? So standing is simply an enforcement or protection or something precious. This is often necessary when examining the meaning of language in-depth, as well as in many other situations. Understanding: to get in depth comprehension.

As the old saying goes, "by all means . . . get an *understanding!*"

LOOKING INSIDE

SHE IS NOT A RAT: UNDERSTANDING WHO A WOMAN REALLY IS

(IF YOU ONLY KNEW HER)

The value of women is so significant yet often underrated and overlooked—I *must* spill the beans on this.

At a service station, a male customer was approached by an unkempt young woman who was begging. He said to her, "Get away from me, you filthy, stinking rat!" So, I approached the man and asked if I could speak to him, to which he replied, "Yes."

I said, "She's not a rat; she's a human. She's a precious woman with a troubled mind. She may look like a rat. She may be *imitating* a rat, but, rest assured, she's not a rat.

Sometimes when a person feels worthless, they may do anything to get attention. They may use foul language. They may dance vulgarly, or they may dress half-naked, all just to feel valuable.

Who knows whether or not some fast-talking 16- or 17-year-old boy talked a hole in her head when she was just 13 or 14 years old, then left her with a baby to raise by herself. That experience might have even repeated itself again and again.

We don't know if that happened or not, but what we *do* know is that something tragic did happen to her. Maybe she had a bad home life or maybe some creepy pimp has her out here right now doing horrible things to her. We really don't know.

Despite those possible setbacks, if you knew her—if you *really* knew her, you'd see she's not a rat. A woman is special. She's the mother of society. Without her contributions, there would be no human beings at all on this earth and inside of her body she possesses the most precious site on Earth. It's called her uterus. It's also called the womb. That's where all humans are developed before being delivered out into the world so that *the rational mind* can be born. Then she teaches us how to eat, changes our stinky diapers, bathes us clean, teaches us to talk and walk, and prepares us for the world's challenges.

She's not a rat. She's somebody, *really* somebody. That dirty, ragged-looking woman over there is precious and needs help. Her distorted mind is doing all these terrible things to her. But if you knew her—if you *really* knew her—you'd *never ever* call her a rat.

There's much, much, good in her. She might not know it or she just doesn't know how to find it. That's because she forgot her own soul. But it's there, waiting for her.

'Appreciate' means '*to increase the value of*'. Maybe we can tell her something of value that we appreciate about her—NOT that rat image. Who knows, that just might be the right thing she needs to jumpstart her life back toward success."

With tears in his eyes, same as I, the man thanked me and said he'd never call anyone a rat again.

SWEETIE

This chapter is longer, but it is a must, and it deserves its place in this book. We are analyzing two words that are pronounced the same but have different spellings and meanings: dessert and desert.

Sweetie refers to "desserts" such as pastries, cakes, and pies, etc. During this discussion, the flavor and taste of sweet desserts refers to physical attraction, and "desert" refers to abandoning appreciation and acknowledgement for the value of a woman's mind. If we allow ourselves to become a sugar junkie that is only in love with physical attraction with little or no regard for the value of a woman's mind...

> We are in big trouble
> We are in a jam
> That means hooked
> That means trapped
> That means caught
> That means lured by a physical magnet called sweetie

A little sweet is okay, but *too much* of this powerful dessert is a trip to looneyville. Check out these terms of endearment:

> *"Hi, sweetie,"*
> *"Come here, sugar,"*
> *"Love you, honey,"*
> *"Sugar plum,"*
> *"Sugar bunch,"*

"Love you, sweetheart,"
"My cupcake,"
"You're my honey dripper."

Here, **the taste and flavor are disguises of the real woman.** A dangerous overdose of sweetie can cause one to lose focus.

The eye-catching clothing, costly makeup, fake hair and eyelashes, bright fingernail and toenail polish, tiptoeing in back damaging high heel shoes are all unnatural contributions to physical attraction. Oh, and let's not leave out the silicon invasion!

Let's take an even closer look at this powerful luring dessert, called physical attraction. It can cause a woman's powerful mind to be overlooked or ignored. When this happens, men might only desire her physical appearance, and begin to worship her body. This can make some men think she's nothing but her body. **Well let's straighten this out *right now.***

Can we agree that women are more than a hold-me-tight, and certainly a whole lot more than just somebody's ol' be my baby tonight? Although she has a precious heart, beautiful eyes and gorgeous lips, she lives in the brain and NOT IN THE HIPS. She is *somebody*, I mean *really* somebody. Women are equal to men. One has a slight edge over the other in terms of natural roles. The natural roles are just different. Any man who thinks otherwise let us see him try to have a baby. Every woman is specially created whether she ever has a baby or not. She has an inherent mother's nature. She can just look at or touch a man a certain way that makes him forget all of his troubles. She gets us going. She's everyone's first teacher; just think about it, she teaches us before anyone else. She gets it done.

Grandmas,
Mothers,
Wives,
Aunts,

Nieces,
Sisters,
Little girls (around the world)
Oh, my goodness, my oh my, you get it done.

There are many wonderful things about you, but you don't get credit for all you do. I'm inviting all men to stand up, putting a light on you, because, today, men need to open our eyes and see, that, *without women*, we would not exist. A man may go out and win half the world, and then forget how he got to it, when, many times, there was a woman somewhere that taught him how to do it. You're somebody, sister! *Really* somebody. Your time is now. Claim your fame!

From the highest mountain, I'd like to hear us men saying:

She's more than a "hold me tight." And she is more than a "be my baby tonight." She has a wonderful heart, gorgeous lips, but, she lives in the brain and not in the hips.

If we men want to really find the real you and get a brand new start, we'll have to look deep into your original human nature, and, there, we'll find **you, and your wonderful heart.**

Beans Spilled.

MISS LADY'S KITCHEN: HOMEMADE FOOD AND A MODEL FOR GOOD BUSINESS SENSE

In my travels I experienced a great restaurant owned and oper-
ated by a woman displaying good business sense. Though
some of the customers may have been strangers, the environment always felt like family. She told the story about how chal-
lenging it was for her because this was her first business and
she knew that she would have to "sink or swim."

It seemed to have wall to wall people every day. People
came continuously to eat. When asked, "How do you explain
the booming business and the huge number of customers that
you sustained for so many years?" She said, "It's simple, I always
taste my food while I'm cooking it and also after I finish cooking it. I am kind to my customers and greet my regular customers by their names. We always make sure all the customers feel
welcome and kindly acknowledge them when they come in and
when they are leaving."

When I say the food is "homemade" I make sure it is homemade because I cook it myself or hire cooks that will allow me
to train them to cook my way from scratch. I tweak the coffee
a little bit so it has a good flavor because people love the taste
of good coffee. I always make sure the food tastes good and I
give them plenty, a healthy helping, and make sure they don't
have a long wait to get served. If someone happens not to finish their plate or leaves a large portion on their plate, I inquire,

"Is there something wrong with the food?" I want to make sure they like what they were served. If there is any flaw in my cooking, I want to correct it. I want to make sure it is up to par all the time, every day.

Her customers sense that and they know she wants to be fair with them. Giving them good quality, good tasting food, and plenty of it along with kind service. She keeps her whole restaurant packed with people all the time. Thumbs up for Miss Lady's Kitchen!

MAMA, DADDY, BABY

S he calls him daddy, he calls her mama, and they both call each other baby. *Wow,* this is so in the pocket. They comfort each other by addressing their original natures.

⊶═◉ ◉═⊷

SISTER GIRL NAILED IT

N ow here is an eye-opening argument:
A man and woman were arguing. He was being very forceful and trying to dominate her, but she stopped him in his tracks. I overheard her saying, "I'll listen to you when you learn how to urinate straight and stop leaving the toilet seat up. I'm tired of mopping up behind you, *bruh.*"

Busted.
Beans Spilled.

HI, DAD

A man was talking to his daughter. He said, "It seems like it was just a moment ago that you and your mother were saying, 'Oh, that stupid fool.' But I just came into a whole lot of money lately, and here you come again with your Academy Awards performance, saying 'Hi, dad, YOU'RE SO COOL!'"

Oops! Does this really happen sometimes?

HE SAID, SHE SAID

H e said, "You don't know what you got. You ain't gonna ever find another one like me!" She said, "Thank God!" *Women and girls around the world agree with her in their own language:*

感謝上帝 (Chinese Traditional)
gracias a Dios (Spanish)
Salamat sa Diyos (Filipino)
godiya ga allah (Hausa)
شكرا يا الله (Arabic)
Dieu merci (French)
Danke Gott (German
תודה לאל (Hebrew)
Asante Mungu (Swahili).

He said, "This ain't no act. I'm gonna be gone longer, then I'm never coming back."
She said, "Would you please put that in writing?!"

HEN PECKED

D o some people not pay attention to what they're saying? Sometimes one can go to the extreme. One person said, "I know she loves me. She protects my privacy. She loves me. I know *she do* because just last night she said, 'Ain't nobody going to know that you're **stupid**, but just me and you.'"

I wonder if either one heard what they said?

-⊷⊨⊜⊨⊷-

SOMETHING FOR NOTHING

W hen someone offers me something for nothing, I usually tell them, "*I can't afford it.*"

MAMA CAN THROW DOWN

A woman is sweet and gentle but has **tiger** *in her, too.* Mama can throw down if she has to.

Example: A big bad bully just stole the show, bragging about how he slapped a woman last week. A woman then came back with a two-by-four and knocked out all of his teeth while shouting, "Kick 'em in the mud, kick 'em in the dirt, get up homie, you ain't hurt!"

Now, see what you got? You got to see the other side of a woman that you didn't know was there. You had it coming. Good for you!

Without any hesitation, the woman composed herself and went right back to that soft, sweet, nurturing side that she also possesses. She turned around, looked at the crowd, and then softly said, *"Hi."*

He just didn't know that mama could throw down.

Beans Spilled.

WHAT A REAL MAN IS
The *"Ain't Taking No Boo Boo"* Giant

Some women will try to walk all over a man but a real man just won't let her. That's because he understands her. He realizes that some bullies might have tried to mistreat her before he ever met her. A real man will say,

"**Let's get rid of that ol' loving for sex alone** *mindset*. Let's make this agreement, and then get it on." A real man says, "It takes two. The lip professor won't do. Let's believe what each other is saying simply because it matches what we see each other do. Then add it to respect and appreciation, mixed with a bond that will not break. You see that I have your back, and I know you have mine. Now that we have a working relationship that we know is true, baby, **if anybody ever** *tries* **to misuse you it ain't no telling what I might do.**

We can now safely say both of us are blessed. With all of this in mind, **we're doing just fine**. *You got yourself a man this time.*

A real man is more than just some muscles. He's a safe haven for a woman. You're sailing now, baby, **you got yourself a man this time.**"

Beans Spilled.

THE WITCH'S BROOM

C an we take a moment? Let's see if we can agree on this. If we men have a good woman we should always treat her right and give her the best. She's better than the rest. A good woman should without fail have a prime place in her man's heart. Because a good woman will come to her man when he's hurt and nurture him back to health. Every man needs that sometimes. A man and his woman are supposed to be close indeed. We're supposed to be so close until when one is cut the other one bleeds.

Are we on the same page? **GOOD!**

So now, let's go to a witch. A witch is a witch and cannot be made into a rose that blooms. She's going to do what she does and is not willing to change anytime soon. A witch will never stop until she sees her man hurt. She won't break stride until she sees him lying in the dirt. A witch loves her broom.

The nature of a broom is to sweep up all that's loose, including the crumbs. Taking everything you've got. But I know of a way to stop a witch. Take away her broom; that will put her in check. Believe it or not.

I knew you had something up your sleeve and you were out to get me. But I took away your broom.

Because when I left, *I took my* WALLET *with me!*

I'M STANDING ON
THE PRINCIPLE

I heard a world-renowned trustworthy scholar, Professor W.D., make this statement. He said the following:

I'm standing on the principle,
not on the pain,
not on the hurt.
One can fight much longer
fighting for the principle
than fighting for the hurt.
After a while,
the pain and hurt might leave,
but there is still a need
to continue the fight
because others are hurting.

Can we agree to stand on the principle.

WORDS MAKE PEOPLE

WORDS MAKE PEOPLE, PART 1

I f words make people, I wonder what these words do to folks?
Here are a few greetings:

Person 1: Hi, what are you up to?
Person 2: Oh, I ain't no good.
Person 1: Hi, how is the world treating you?
Person 2: It's your world, I'm just living in it.
Person 1: What do you know, dude?
Person 2: Oh, I don't know it.
Person 1: How've you been doing?
Person 2: If I had your hand, I'd throw mine away.
Person 1: Last night I got torn down—I mean I got f'ed up!
       I don't know who brought me home.
Person 2: Are you sure you want to brag about that?
Person 1: And tomorrow night I'm going back again!
Person 2: Are you really sure you want to brag about that?

A missed-communication greeting:

What are two people thinking when they greet the following way? One opens the greeting with the term, *good morning,*
and the other one replies by saying, "*Fine, fine! And you?*"

WHAT? They are saying two completely different things.
One person is simply saying *good morning,* and the other one
responded with an unrelated answer, "*Fine, fine! and you?* This
indicates there is a miscommunication here. We all make innocent mistakes sometimes, that's just human error. It's not the

end of the world it just appears to be a mistake. No one asked the replying person about personal affairs.

Hmm, very interesting. Good communication is important.

Beans Spilled.

WORDS MAKE PEOPLE, PART 2

I wonder what these words do to us? Putting low filthy things in high clean places using inappropriate language.

Some examples:

Holy f---ng Jesus!
Holy f---ng Christ!
Holy f--k!

Having exciting sex and shouting, *"OMG!"*
Was that the wrong place to use that sacred term? Plus, they might not have even been with their spouse!

Hmm, interesting . . .

This doesn't appear to have reason involved. Could it be that they simply aren't thinking clearly?

WORDS MAKE PEOPLE, PART 3

A man walked up to me and asked, "How are you feeling?"
I replied, "With every sense I have."
He said, "You know what I mean. I mean how are you doing?"
I replied, "How am I doing what?"
He said, "Let me put it this way: How is she going?"
I replied, "By plane."
He said, "Are we really that far off?"
I said, "It appears that way."
He replied, "Good grief."
I asked, "Why call grief good?"
He said, "Holy s-h-i-t."
I said, "Look what you just called holy."
The man thanked me. I appreciated him for understanding.
I responded with a, "Thank you."
He quickly responded back by saying, "You bet."
I said "Who me? I don't gamble." (*chuckling*) The man agreed with me and said, "I'll have to remember that."

Are we really communicating or are we just making sounds? What would happen if we actually answered most greetings that we're given correctly? If we say what we mean, it might be a shock to experience clear communication!

UNDERSTANDING "BASED ON A TRUE STORY"

I think a few beans need to be spilled on this. The phrase, **"based** on a true story" **does not necessarily mean** *that the story is true*. The characters may be real but the story is not. It does not say that this is a true story. It says that it is *based* on one or a hint of one. A composer can invent a false story and use "based on a true story" as a marketing tool to make a great false story appear to be true so that it is marketable, sellable. Did we go for that? Maybe we used to, but no more.

The beans have been spilled.

DAMN RIGHT

D id you ever notice two people agreeing on a good point, and then cursing that good point saying,

"Damn right!"

Why curse what is right (i.e., correct)? Did right do anything to you?

⋆⇒○⇐⋆

UNAWARE COMPLIMENT

T he intended insult "You **ain't** nothing!" is actually a compliment. The word "nothing" means empty, no significance, and/or worthless. The *real* insult would be to say that, "You **are** nothing!" because this means one doesn't have substance. "You ain't nothing!" is actually saying that you are NOT empty, of no significance and/or worthless. In fact, it means that you DO have substance.

CURSING ONE'S SELF

Have you ever witnessed someone getting angry at another person and cursing their own self out by saying,

"Well, I'll be damned."

Are we giving that any thought? Are we damning ourselves?

⊷⊨◉ ◉⊨⊶

WOW, LOOK AT THIS! HELLO!

Are we aware that greeting each other with "hello" is wishing each other *hell* and *low* before we get started? Let's have a look. The "w" is missing in *low*. But, in the pronunciation? *Bingo!* Hello is saying hell and low.

Wow, you just cursed someone out with hell and low, then said "Nice to see you!"

Interesting . . .

Unconsciously, we're putting hell and low in a high place. Maybe the greetings:

Good morning,
Good afternoon, or
Good evening

would be better. More refreshing. *What do you think?*

Beans Spilled.

ENTER-RESTING

(INTERESTING)

A unique way to view the word "interesting" is to consider the phrase, "enter-resting"; it means to pause before continuing or starting again. If one is concentrating on something and is distracted, the present thought is put on hold, enters rest, by the distraction. After that experience, one leaves the distraction and then returns to the previous thoughts and activities.

The natural world is an open book; let's read a few pages. What do you think?

AMAZING GRACE

Did you ever imagine that words from a song could be so powerful? The meaning of "Amazing Grace" became even more powerful to me when I discovered something I didn't see before, separating the sentimental melody from the precious lyrics.

"Amazing Grace." "Grace" is amazing when applied to clean, positive, organized thoughts. Its calm, soothing, healing powers are a mighty statement all of its own. I see grace here much like the smooth movements of a skilled ballerina or the eloquent sounds played by a well-rounded violinist. It's like the quiet calmness of one praying in solitude. That grace is amazing because of what it can do.

Now let's go further and examine "how sweet the sound." I was able to see that "sweet" here represents addiction to the sound. Not the literal sound my ears hear, but the **sound logic** (the truth, i.e., something well put together), and that sound logic is what "saved a wretch like me" (not wreck mind you, but w-r-e-t-c-h). "Wretch" means disorganized. Grace saved a wretch like me.

Now, let's get some goose bumps. There's another part that's very, very important. "I once was lost"—lost from what? "Lost" here refers to one forgetting the source. "But now I'm found"—wow, meaning re-membered, we're back home and back together again by remembering Grace (the soul). Now that we have our foundation (found-*day*-tion) back, one can start all over again. But only if we're sincere about the huge gift called Amazing Grace (the soul)."

WHAT CONNECTS TIME AND DETERMINATION?

What is time? Time is a measurement of a fixed term. Minutes, seconds, hours, days, weeks, months, and so on are examples of time.

Let's examine a meaning for *"de-term-i-nation."*

The prefix here is "de"

"De" means to undo or carry out

"Term" means a fixed period of time

"I" means an individual

"Nation" indicates the independent package, concept, idea, community, country, and/or philosophy in an independent package.

Therefore, the one meaning for "determination" is to carry out in a timely fashion an individual's concept/idea to the end of a fixed term.

THE WORLD'S LONGEST PREGNANCY

A merica is still pregnant, carrying an undelivered baby called *Democracy*. Will our well-intended prayers and rational hard work lead to a healthy delivery?

Reality or myth?

Who is "We The People"? Is it one group or is it many independent groups named "We The People"?

Who is "The Majority Rules"? Is it one group or is it many independent groups named "The Majority Rules"?

So, what "We The People" are we talking about? And what is "The Majority Rules" that we are speaking of?

Beans Spilled.

SUCCESS

THE GIRL WHO WOULDN'T QUIT

Beans spilled all over the place with *this* story:

There is a young woman that we've known since birth. She always studied hard in school from kindergarten to high school and college. When she arrived at college, she didn't slow down, she didn't back off. She had that same drive. She would say to herself, "If *I am to succeed, I have to stay curious and persevere.*"

She graduated with honors before going on to teach middle school science for a year while simultaneously completing a Master of Education and Teaching Credential program. But she didn't stop there; she continued on to receive a Master of Science in Biochemistry and Molecular Biology. Some wondered if she had become a *professional student.* No, this young woman had higher goals in mind. Returning to teach middle school science for another year she, eagerly awaited acceptance to medical school.

Guess what? Once again, she graduated with honors with her medical degree to go directly to her first residency program in pediatrics. Next was a residency program in anesthesiology at an elite institution. She then was granted a fellowship in a pediatric anesthesiology program at a prestigious teaching hospital. Now she works as a medical problem solver and practitioner.

We were on the phone the other day and I asked her, "How are you doing, baby?" She said, "Oh, I'm just trying to figure it out." I said, "You will. Just think about the journey you've already made. Medically speaking back at the point of conception from 15 to 200 million sperm were released and out of all those sperm released only one made it to the egg and fertilized it and you were uniquely created. So you are no wimp, you will nail it." She said, "Wow I did do that didn't I?" I said, "Yes, but it doesn't stop there. Look how you were able to leap over hurdle after hurdle in school. Look how you were able to pick the most precious young man for your husband and now you are going to be a mom soon. When you said to me you were just trying to figure it out, I wanted to do cartwheels because I know you will. Young woman, you are no wimp, you are a hurdler. Don't worry you're blessed with success already in you. I repeat you are not a wimp. You've done it, you are doing it and still reaching."

"Life is an open book as we know and you read it very well. You are an inspiration to many already; you're right on schedule. When the goal is right you hold on tight. You keep your focus, you're a giant in every sense of the word. And just because you are you, you'll figure it out."

PRACTICE

There was an old man in the neighborhood who was asked by a young man, "How can I better myself." The old man said, "Well son every journey starts with the first step whether it's five miles or a thousand miles, it always begins with the first step." The young man responded, "I still don't get it." The old man said, "I'm going to see if I can get you going with one word, **"practice"**.

When you choose a new goal for yourself drop your old habits." "How do I get rid of my old habits?" The boy asked. "**Practice**, persevere, do it over and over again. You can look back at your old habits and say to yourself everyday:

'If I stop thinking like that,
I won't do like that,
If I stop doing like that,
I won't be like that!'"

The old man continued, "The more you **practice** something the easier it becomes. The easier something is to do the more we like it."

ROAD MAP TO SUCCESS

Admiring another person's success is okay sometimes. But it is *not* okay to forget about mine. My success should be very important to me. It should be so important that I never forget to plan and try. Because, if I don't plan, and if I don't try, I can kiss real success goodbye.

Only admiring someone else's achievements is not the way. We must plan; we must try. No one can ever get in shape sitting in the window, watching joggers run by.

Now here's the plan. Here's the simple formula, proven to work. It's on the golden map called "the Road Map to Success."

What if we say let's remove any negative, crippling habits? What if we ask ourselves with this in mind, should we waste our valuable time learning unnecessary things that we don't need to learn? All of the sports scores, the next dance steps or moves, the handful of curse words that exist? The answer is *no!*

Shouldn't we be grateful for being able to learn in the first place? Then and *only then* we must learn how to choose a positive goal. Next, we must find and learn the correct plan that will take us to that goal. Learn that, then do it. Applying it is a must. *Then* we'll be rolling up the road to real success.

A renowned scholar once told me, "If you intend to reach your goal, you must be headed in that direction." So, there we have it: the simple formula, *"The Road Map to Success."*

BYE

I remember a kind old man we all loved and called, "Uncle Joe." He was always organizing, putting things into perspective, and getting things done. He was a winner. Even when he became very old, he was still remarkable. He learned how to operate his mobile phone, and he learned the basics of operating his computer.

One day I asked him, "Uncle Joe, how did you come to be like this? How are you able to achieve all this?" And this is what he told me:

"Son, if I don't try, BYE! If I don't get up and shake the cobwebs and go again, I'll never know what might have been. So, you see, my boy, if I don't try, it's bye.

For anyone to have courage, there has to exist a monster called opposition. So, I never put the monster in "save," and there's no "undo." I tell "disappointment" I delete you! If we don't try, BYE! It's night-night. It's sleep tight. It's just BYE.

I have to throw some lefts and rights sometimes. But I embrace good wherever I find it. Then achievement becomes my friend. If I know for sure that I'm right, I never become afraid to try again. It's mine for the taking but I can't be faking. I have to be true to what I believe and what I'm doing. I don't put the monster in save. In fact, it's true, I tell disappointment, I'm not going back because I deleted you. Now is it clear, my boy? *If I don't try, bye!*"

Uncle Joe Y. Wilson is my hero. "Wow, if I don't try, BYE! I'll never forget you, Uncle Joe."

SO TRUE

Whatever we do, we get some more of that. It's called *rehearsing.* If we do nothing, we get some *more* nothing and go *down, down, down.*

If a car is not used for a long time, the tires will go flat. You must use the car.

If a house is abandoned for a long time, the roof will fall in. You must use the house.

If I don't succeed, often times that means I've been practicing failure. We definitely get some more of whatever we do.

A CHOICE

D id you know that one has to work to be lazy? One has to work really hard doing more nothing to earn more laziness. Some people will trade clear guidance for error. Do you agree, that we should always have good intentions, supported by reason and good work, to obtain victory?

LESSONS LEARNED

THE ONE BISCUIT

S hortly before my sister, Robbie, passed away, she reminded me of something that happened when we were children that impacted and enhanced her life.

Robbie said, "I'll get right to the point . . . Do you remember, one day at school, there was a girl who came from a family far out in the country? They struggled and were very, very poor. When it was time for lunch at school, this little country girl opened a "Brother Rabbit" syrup can, and all she had in that syrup can was *one biscuit*.

I thought that was hilarious, and I laughed at the little girl. The little girl started crying because I teased her by repeatedly saying, 'All you have to eat is one biscuit, ha-ha-ha.' I thought it was so funny. I continued to tease the girl about having only one biscuit to eat, and she ate her one biscuit as she continued to cry.

Remember when we got home from school that day and grandmother ("Mama") was waiting? Mama said to me, 'Let's hear about this one biscuit business at school today.' I started laughing hysterically, saying, 'Mama, all she had to eat was one biscuit, ha-ha-ha.' Mama responded, 'You should never do that. Here's what I want you to do; first, I want you to go and apologize to that girl.' I was shocked. 'Then', Mama said, 'you'll also invite that girl and her whole family here for dinner'.

That night, that little girl I laughed at and her whole family were seated at our long dinner table, where Mama had the food laid out the way Mama knew how to do it. Everybody's plates were loaded, and the table was full of food.

But, on my plate, there was just *one biscuit.* So, I said, 'Mama, all I have is one biscuit.' Mama said, 'That's all you get is one biscuit, and that's so you'll never forget how it feels to be in the middle of people who have plenty and you don't. You'll know how it feels when someone laughs at you for no reason other than the fact that you're poor. You'll always remember that. While everyone else is enjoying their plate full of food, you eat your one biscuit.'

I never forgot that lesson, and I never ever laughed at anybody else again who was lacking something. Contrary to that, I always try to help those who are in need."

I said to my sister, "I do the same thing, Robbie, and so did our brother, Donnie, before he left us. We all help those who don't have. I think that's because of our grandmother, Hannah "Mama" Collins' guidance, and the guidance of our grandfather, Wallace Collins. We're blessed to have had grandparents like that. You never forgot that one biscuit, Robbie. Donnie, and I never forgot it either. Look what that one biscuit did!"

WONDER WHY

Have you ever considered that fireworks sound like war to some people? The sounds of war are all around us with the exploding fireworks on holidays and celebrations. Some of us might take these beautiful sights for granted. Others may not see the beautiful colors and flurries of light. They only hear the deafening firework explosions while staying inside their homes clinging tightly to each other. These sounds remind them of the bombs and horror they may have endured in their native lands. They panic from fright just from the memories related to the sounds of war they have experienced.

A LESSON LEARNED
Food Pre-Seasoning

I was in a restaurant when I overheard a woman talking to a man. They were sitting at the next table over from me. She said to him, "It appears to me that you're not accustomed to the taste of good quality food."

The man responded bitterly by saying he was insulted and asked why she said that.

She replied, "Because you always carry a little bottle of hot sauce with you when we go out. Before you even taste one bite of the food, you season it. You salt and pepper it, and you put your personal hot sauce all over it. If it's a steak, and we're paying $75 per person for the meal, the chef has taken pride and worked hard to make those steaks taste just right. Before you sample a single taste, you put salt and pepper on it, and you also add steak sauce. Without fail, out of your pocket comes a little bottle of Tabasco sauce. So that tells me you must not be used to good-quality and good-tasting food. You feel so sure it doesn't taste right, that you must help it, even before you begin to eat."

The man did something I didn't expect. He put away his hot sauce, reached across the table, and gently held her hands. With a loving look on his face, he said respectfully, "Thank you, baby."

After I heard them, I wondered how many times I had done the same thing myself. I noticed that I had my salt shaker in my hand. I put my salt shaker down. In my heart, I quietly thanked that couple.

MY FATHER TALKING
TO HIS WORKERS

M y father was talking to his workers one day, and he said, "I've tried to always contribute to the best of society." One of his workers, an arrogant guy, asked, "And just how in the hell are ya supposed to do that?" My dad said, "I lock up everything that I possibly can . . . from *your* ass."

Nuff said.
Beans Spilled.

MY GRANDDADDY

When I was a boy in Texas, I thought my grandfather was the meanest person in the world. I literally hated him and thought he hated me. It wasn't until I paid some dues, that I developed real love and appreciation for him, and all of the guidelines he instilled in my brother, my sister, and me.

He said,
"To make it in this world, you first have to trust divine guidance and then learn the territory that you're getting into."

He said,
"Always try to first understand something about what you're getting yourself into before you get yourself into it."

He would say, *"Always do your job well."*

He had a saying,
"Don't give me no 'that'll do!'" Then he would check the job, and it had better be done well.

He would repeatedly say,
"Don't lie, and don't steal."

He would say,
"If I ever find out you've been lying or stealing, I'll quit putting out a fire to come whip your behind."

At the time, I thought all his sayings were terrible. But, until this day, I try not to lie. I do not steal. I try hard to do my job well. I've made many mistakes in this life—and still do today—but every day is cleanup day for me.

Today, I often think of my granddaddy and wish he was alive, so I could go to him, give him a big hug, and say,

"Granddaddy, I really, really appreciate you now."

So, today, I'm spilling the beans, saying "Now I know. I get the point! Thank you, Granddaddy. I sure wish you were here to see me doing what you asked me to do."

Thank you, Papa. We thank the Most High for you.

I just spilled the beans.

PROFESSOR HUMPHREY
THE SCIENTIST

Proof is not bad. Its evidence establishes a fact or facts.
Example: There was a man (respecting his family we won't reveal his name) who was arrogant and thought he was huge. He became furious when someone told him he was small. It led to an investigation by a curious scientist by the name of Professor Humphrey.

The accused man had a lot of money that he used to manipulate other people just to watch them fall. Professor Humphrey, the scientist, said, "I accept the challenge to fairly look into this. If a fact or facts are not present, a scientist doesn't believe it." The truth is in the proof. After careful observation, Professor Humphrey said to the boasting one, "I've completed my investigation, and here are my results."

"Look at what you say. It's different from what you do. The answer is simply this: you're not so big after all. I've come to find out you're just tall; that's all. The people who you make feel small in reality may be bigger than you."

Everything in this world is not peaches and cream. But be hopeful because there are peaches and cream available.

THE AMAZING ANATOMY

NOSY

O ne of our many senses is the nose. So often we overlook it. But the nose is helpful. Each nostril smells different scents than the other one, and each nostril can decipher over a trillion different scents. We could never enjoy the taste of food without the nose.

We're rarely conscious of the sense of smell. After the nose gives us a hunch, we might say,

"That was right under my nose," or
"I smell trouble," or
"I smell a rat," or
"I had a feeling that was going to happen."

The nose sensed that feeling before the mind caught it and gave it to us in the way of feelings.

The word "k-n-o-w-s" means "divine inspiration."

After a purchase, we might say,

"They charged me through the nose for that!"

Meaning: we learned a lesson from that experience which will benefit and hopefully protect us from paying through the nose again. We *earn* some information by *paying* for it with attention. So, pay through the nose.

Even in the movies, in the cartoons, they show a woman purposely drop her handkerchief as she meets a guy. When the guy sees the handkerchief falling, a propeller on his cap starts spinning wildly as he does flips and cartwheels. The purposely dropped handkerchief here strongly implies *"she got him by the nose."*

The human nose is so sensitive that even the physically strongest person could be held flat on their back on the floor if another person holds a small piece of thread tightly underneath their nose because it feels like the thread is razor-sharp and will cut their nose. In reality, it cannot. It can be easily broken if the person sits up. But they usually cannot sit up because the nose makes them afraid.

One of the ways the nose protects itself is by making the person afraid. An animal protects the physical weakness of its precious nose by growling, showing you his teeth to take your attention away from his nose. The nose is so vulnerable that if you put a ring in the nose of a wild bull and put a rope through the nose ring, a little child could take up the rope and lead the bull through the town.

We cannot enjoy a pleasant meal without the nose and its many receptors. The nose saves our lives by saying, "Don't eat that; it's spoiled!" We could be asleep and the nose might wake us up by saying, "Hey, wake up! Do you know your house is on fire?" The nose has many functions. We should always be grateful for the nose.

Even though our nose has many sensory receptors, a dog has over a million more receptors than humans. A dog's sense of smell is so keen that they can smell footsteps or body scents even days after a person has left an area. A rat or a mouse can smell food left out on the stove or counter from several blocks away.

We are thankful for the nose. Just think about what one is missing who has never smelled the fresh air in the springtime.

I just spilled the beans!
Guess I was being nosy . . .

OUR MIGHTY FIVE
AND MORE SENSES

D id you know that the only way to connect to the outside world is through our senses? The senses have trillions of intermingling networks that we never hear about. Receptor signals must pass through these networks for us to make a concept or picture of anything we want to perceive.

No sense. No perception. No sense. No pictures. No sense. No info.

It is a common belief that we only have five senses, but actually we have many more senses. All of our other senses are connected to the five main senses. It is important to recognize and take good care of our senses by rehearsing them. We do this by paying attention to what each sense does and how it improves through repeated usage. Repetition helps us improve our ability to cultivate our perception.

Examples of senses that are not the five main senses include the sense of balance, the sense of direction, the sense of time, the sense of fear, the sense of happiness, the sense of judgment, the sense of distance, the sense of humor, the sense of pressure, and many more.

The sense of memory is strongly connected to the sense of smell. Have you ever smelled perfume or cologne and been reminded of someone? Have you ever smelled fresh-baked cookies and been reminded of mom, aunt, or grandma?

The sixth sense is important too. The sixth sense is not as easy to classify. It refers specifically to our ability to make decisions about our five main senses such as what sense to use, when to use a sense, and how much of that sense to use.

So now that we know that the only way for us to communicate with the outside world is through our senses, this explains why it is so important for us not to get overly emotional. Too much emotion can distort perception. Our senses need tender love and care. If we do that, then we can say with confidence, "That makes sense!"

Identifying and using *all* of our senses is exciting, and it makes sense to do so! Scientific researchers say if we use our senses more, then we can obtain better benefits. What do you think? There's much more information on this matter that sparked my curiosity to investigate; if you care to do the scientific research on it and more, you may be very happy.

Yay for the senses!

PAIN TO THE RESCUE

I remember when I was a boy my grandmother lost her sense of feeling on one side of her body. Being numb on that side left her vulnerable to cutting, burning or fracturing her bones. One day when she was ironing clothes she burned her arm really, really bad but didn't know her arm was stuck to the iron burning until she smelled it. The rest of her life the reminder of her loss of the sense of pain was a huge scar on her arm. That gave me a great appreciation for the purpose of pain and what the sense of pain can do.

Pain has never been the problem; pain warns us there is a problem. Much like the burglar alarm, the alarm has never been the burglar. It alerts us to the presence of the intruder. Pain is a language or signal that talks to us. Sometimes pain will make us want to talk back to it! We might yell "Pain you just said something." We might say, "Pain, you said a mouthful that time" or "Pain, you just pulled my coat." I wouldn't have known I was in trouble, if it hadn't been for you." Can we say that natural pain is our friend?

Can we actually appreciate something we hate? I found this to be true. We hate pain because it hurts so badly but we should appreciate pain because its purpose is good. All pain that we experience alerts us to something that needs to be dealt with or removed and then the pain will go away.

Natural pain is good; provoked pain may not be good. An example of provoked pain is self-inflicted pain when we force our body repeatedly to endure excruciating pain to test our physical limits. If we do this repeatedly there is great danger and sometimes death. That is an unnatural use of pain. Over taxing our body and ignoring the signals of pain is a huge risk.

On the other hand, natural pain shows up without warning to alert us of a danger that needs to be repaired. Remember the difference in provoked pain and natural pain. Can we then give a big *"thank you"* for our friend natural pain? Pain **will** definitely get our attention.

THE LIPS ARE NO JOKE

THE LIPS

W*hat would we do without lips?* Do we ever think of the importance of our lips? Well, let's have a look. They're right under our nose; we're just not paying attention to them. Where else can they be? They're not in our pockets!

We usually forget about learning how to talk. It was not an easy process to learn how to talk. There are many combinations of things that have to take place for a person to talk.

Can we try a quick test? First, open the mouth, then hold the top and bottom lips with the index and thumb fingers of each hand and try to say the word "mama." Ha-ha-ha, impossible! It's wonderful!

Do we appreciate all the gifts we've been given? Hmmm, interesting. Somehow, we seem to forget all about them. *The lips are no joke!* If you don't mind, with your permission, I'd like to share a few things that we may know, we may not know, or we have forgotten.

Without the lips, we can't even say the word, "baby." We can't say "please," we can't say "never," and don't even try to say "me," without those precious lips. The lips are one of the most sensitive and important parts in our body. Our lips have a network of nerves and receptors right near the outer surface. The lips have over one million receptors that transmit information to the brain and other places. The lips are vital to keeping a tight seal so we can swallow. The lips form the sounds of "m," "b," and "p," but the lips must come together to do it. To make the sound "f" or even make the sound "v," our lower lip must touch the upper teeth. There are many other things the lips must do just to talk. Imagine trying to drink a glass of water with no lips, *no way*! And don't even imagine trying to eat a bowl of rice with no lips, no way.

KISSING

Just saying or thinking of saying, "Hi, mom" is heartwarming. With mom, ooh we feel so comfortable, so protected, so secure. Our first experiences with love and security are usually associated with lips. Signals from the brain stimulate the baby's behaviors that imitate kissing. Nursing is the main one, and so is bottle feeding. These experiences send information about positive emotions to the brain that stay with a person for a lifetime.

I repeat, our lips have over *one million* receptors and are so sensitive, according to scientists, that the slightest touch sends an enormous amount of information to the brain, and that can make us feel super good. A very large part of the brain is activated by kissing because it is associated with sensory information. Kissing sets off a huge number of neurotransmitters and hormones throughout our bodies. Wow, that's why we think like "this" or think like "that."

Scientific research has found that, when two lovers are kissing, they transmit or exchange at least 80 million bacteria, but surprisingly most are not bad.

When we kiss passionately, it can increase the neurotransmitter, dopamine. Dopamine is tied to cravings and desire, but oxytocin is known as the "love hormone." Oxytocin causes a sense of closeness and attachment. Another hormone is adrenaline. Adrenaline boosts the heart rate and causes sweating that allows one lover to smell the other one and make a decision as to whether they want to go further.

While passionately kissing, we get to know a lot about the other person because the noses are so close together. We learn a lot about each other from the sense of smell, taste, and touch.

All of these signals trigger other signals, so the lips are NO joke.

Scientific research has also determined that most people prefer to kiss other people before having sexual intercourse with them. This is because of what they can learn about the other person through taste, smell, and touch. The lip receptors are so sensitive that they can instantly cause a chain reaction. They can trigger thrills throughout the body, almost like magic.

Another interesting point is that the lips' receptors can send signals to the brain to get the brain to overlook activity that is taking place at the time of great pleasure. That is the act of putting spit in each other's mouth—or spit swapping. These pleasures override the consciousness of the disgusting act of mixing spit in each other's mouths. The kissing exchange, however, feels so good that we start not to mind the spit. Putting spit in another's mouth is very normal. Birds do it. Chickens do it. Humans do it. Some mothers chew up the food first then put it into their baby's mouth. Spit breaks the food up, and the mother puts the spit-filled food in the baby's mouth. So, with that being said, it's normal for lovers to do it. It's natural to have all these checks and balances. So, yay to the kissing. We're not dropping the kissing. YAY to the lips! What would we do without lips? If you can hold your lips and say "mama" I won't say anymore.

READER PARTICIPATION

Let's take a brief break and try something. Let's have some fun. Hold your lips together and try to say the following words out loud:

Try to say "hop"
Try to say "stop"
Try to say "pop"
Try to say "never"

Try to say "artificial"
Try to say "demolition"
Try to say "superficial"
Try to say "I love you baby"
Try to say "I'll be back"
Try to say "my, my, my"

Here's another one: *try to say "I love my lips."* Just a little lip appreciation exercise. We cannot speak aloud while holding our lips together. We have to have our lips working.

Now, let's try saying the word, "Victor." Notice the top front teeth must touch the top of the lower lip to say "Vic." The tongue must pop off the roof of the mouth to say "tor." Now we've said, "Victor."

Let's try these words, "much more ice cream." Notice the combination of lip movements that must take place just to say "much more ice cream."

Let's try, "Paul." Bring both lips inward, touching the upper and lower front teeth. Now pop both lips forward and lightly touch the roof of the mouth with the tongue. Now we've said, "Paul."

Wow, those mighty lips!
We can't drink without the lips.
We can't eat without the lips.
We can't talk well without the lips.
We can't sing without the lips.
We can't whistle without the lips.
We can't "sing pop goes the weasel"
We can't say maybe.
We can't kiss without the lips.

We would not have all our great singers if they didn't know how to manipulate their lips so well. Many people cause excitement just by the appearance of their lips. No lips = no great singers.

Do you now agree that the lips are no joke? Scientists who specialize in lip analysis can read lips and can also read our personalities because our lips usually expose our interests. The lips do many things—talking, eating, laughing, kissing, singing, whistling, moaning, smiling, whispering, sucking, and spitting, just to name a few. They can also show kindness, anger, fright, sadness, and happiness.

SCIENTIFIC RESEARCH

According to scientific researchers, we often notice a person's lips first. The shape of our lips decides how we relate to one another. How the lips look reflects our temperament. The way we use words, and the way we speak, exposes our level of confidence. People who are deaf also know how to read lips. That should be enough for now, but there's much, much more. *The lips are no joke!*

TOES

H ave you ever thought of how important toes are to humans and all other living creatures that have them? My doctor informed me of how vital they are. If you have any doubt about how much we depend on our toes, imagine trying to walk, climb, or drive without them.

The big toes are especially important! They are power-ful, support our body weight, and balance our body. Boxers depend on them and gymnasts need them, as is the case for many other athletes.

Toes get their name from their ability to tow the body. We usually don't think much about toes, but they are *quiet giants!*

EPILOGUE
Appreciation

Appreciation means "increased in value" and can also be called "cultivated," as with gardening. Appreciation is the opposite of depreciation. Depreciation means reduced in value. If we buy a new car, as soon as we drive it off the lot, the new car has depreciated (lost value). If we don't keep our house painted and yard maintained, our real estate property loses value, and that's called depreciation.

Appreciation means recognition and enjoyment of the good qualities of someone or something. If we listen to people when they're talking and do something later to let them see we're listening, that cultivates appreciation. Common forms of effective appreciation are to give a simple heartfelt thank you or just simply do something to brighten someone's day. Writing a note to show that we genuinely honor someone's valuable time, and/or something they've shared with us is another way to show appreciation to that person.

If we want a particular behavior to repeat, that behavior needs to be cultivated, rewarded, and pampered. Then the chance of that particular behavior repeating will most likely increase.

Be on time. Keep your promises.

So, there we are, experiencing appreciation in action. Can we agree that appreciation is important because it "raises the value?"

So, there we have it.

Rodger Collins just spilled the beans.

Now that the journey through *Spilling the Beans* concludes, I sincerely hope the reader (no matter where you are, how old you are, your gender, your ideological philosophies, your social status) has gained something that enriches your journey. I sincerely hope you enjoyed reading it as much as I did writing it.

Spilling The Beans - A Book For The World
Rodger Collins

NOTES

Look for future works and information from Rodger Collins
On the website: www.spillingthebeans.com
Email: info@spillingthebeans.com